mean
margaritas
and other tequila cocktails

mean
margaritas
and other tequila cocktails

ben reed

photography by
william lingwood

LONDON · NEW YORK

Senior Designer Toni Kay
Editor Rebecca Woods
Head of Production Patricia Harrington
Art Director Leslie Harrington
Editorial Director Julia Charles

Mixologist Ben Reed
Indexer Hilary Bird

First published in 2012
by Ryland Peters & Small
20–21 Jockey's Fields
London WC1R 4BW
and
Ryland Peters & Small, Inc.
519 Broadway, 5th Floor
New York, NY 10012

www.rylandpeters.com

The recipes in this book have been published
previously by Ryland Peters & Small.

10 9 8 7 6 5 4 3 2

ISBN: 978 1 84975 205 3

A CIP record for this book is available from the
British Library.

Library of Congress Cataloging-in-Publication Data

Reed, Ben.
 Mean margaritas : and other tequila cocktails /
Ben Reed ; photography by William Lingwood. –
1st U.S. ed.
    p. cm.
 Rev. ed. of: Margaritas and other tequila cocktails.
2003.
 Includes index.
 ISBN 978-1-84975-205-3
 1. Margaritas. 2. Tequila. 3. Cocktails. I. Reed,
Ben. Margaritas and other tequila cocktails. II.
Title.
 TX951.R35522 2012
 641.87'4–dc23
                                                  2011035884

Printed in China

Notes

• When using slices of citrus fruit such as lemons
or oranges in a drink, try to find organic, unwaxed
fruits and wash well before using. If you can only
find treated fruit, scrub well in warm soapy water
and rinse before using.

• Measurements are occasionally given in
barspoons, which are equivalent to 5 ml or
1 teaspoon. All recipes make one margarita.

contents

tequila history

Tequila and tequila-based cocktails have always had, how shall I put this, a bit of a reputation. Tequila is the drink of Mexico and perhaps it is the country's turbulent history that lends this drink its roguish image. This was certainly the case during the Mexican revolution, when men wearing bandaleros, sombreros and large moustaches sipped tequila in times of exaltation or catastrophe. Retaining its tempestuous past, tequila has moved on and can be seen today decorating the back bars of cantinas, style bars, pubs, clubs and hotel bars alike.

People everywhere are drinking tequila – from the best-known tequila brands to the rarer tequilas revered by connoisseurs. Tequila has planted itself firmly in the consciousness of the global drinks market and is respected and adored all over the world.

Tequila's origins in Mexico were humble. Approximately 70 per cent of Mexico's territory has an arid or semi-desert climate in which a vast variety of plants grow. The majority of these plants were 'magueys' – later known as 'agave' – which were used for many purposes by the pre-hispanic American people. Clothes and household utensils

were created using the fibres of the plant, but more importantly (for our purposes anyway) they used the sap as a beverage.

I may as well, at this early stage, clear up a fallacy surrounding tequila. The agave plant is not a cactus, despite its appearance, but a member of the lily genus. Within its mass of sharp spiny stems lies the heart (or piña). When pierced, the pineapple-shaped centre releases a sap that you can drink. Leave the liquid for a few hours, however, and it starts to

regulations, similar to those of Champagne and Cognac. According to the Mexican government, tequila must be made from the juice of agave plants grown in one of five Mexican states, contain at least 51 per cent pure agave juice, and be distilled twice.

With the advent of distillation, the method of production has been modernized. Today, the hearts of the agave plant are heated by steam at a very high temperature for up to a day and a half. These hearts are crushed to

the agave plant is not a cactus, despite its appearance, but a member of the lily genus

ferment and turn into alcohol. This alcoholic version of agave juice was called pulque and for the next three hundred years was the traditional drink of Mexico. Tequila was to arrive later on the scene.

Years before the invention of distillation, indigenous farmers discovered their own method of producing alcohol. The jimadors (agave harvesters) would discard the remains of the large plants into deep pits. The story goes that one day a fire started in one of the pits and the heat transformed the plant juice into an alcoholic drink named mezcal.

All tequila is mezcal but not all mezcal is tequila. Tequila production is subject to

release the juice, which is then fermented. The fermented liquid is filtered to rid the mixture of the fibrous residue and any other impurities. Once done, the must (resultant liquid) is ready for distillation.

Modern-day distillation takes place in huge stills into which steam is pumped. Often the wash is processed twice to ensure distillation is thorough. The steam forces the alcohol up through the vat into a type of spout, where it is chilled and collected.

When the tequila leaves the still it is clear looking. This type of tequila is called blanco (white) or plata (silver). It is from this form that the various types of tequila are made.

'Gold' tequila is called *joven abocado* in Mexico (roughly translated as 'young and medium sweet'). The only difference between 'gold' and 'white' tequila is the addition of colouring and a small amount of sweetening agent – often caramel – which both colours and sweetens the drink.

The best-quality tequilas are aged in wooden containers. The official terms for these tequilas are reposado (rested) and añejo (aged). Tequilas described as 'rested' must, somewhat confusingly, also be aged but for a shorter period of time. These tequilas sit in large wooden tanks, some holding as much as 30,000 litres, for a minimum of two months. After two months the tequila can be called reposado but more often they are left for four to eight months (anything up to one year is acceptable). Añejo tequila is any tequila that has been aged for more than a year in wooden tanks or barrels.

The type of barrel used for ageing has a huge effect on the resultant tequila. The barrel's age and previous use (some tequila producers use barrels previously used by whisky makers) are both important as they impart different flavours to the drink. Others experiment with oak barrels or barrels charred on the inside to create their distinctive taste (new barrels have the most flavour).

After ageing, the tequila is prepared for bottling. With both aged and rested tequilas, blending is commonplace. As is the case with blended whisky, the age of the youngest blend used in the mix will be the age of the total blend printed on the bottle. It is the job of the master blender to maintain the consistency of the various tequilas. Taste, appearance and aroma are the three main variables, and although taste and appearance can be altered by using additives, to get the aroma spot on the blender has to rely on one thing: his or her nose.

Next, the tequila is bottled and labelled. The bottles can be as colourful and exciting as the drink itself but be warned: expensive tequila is sometimes priced according to the intricacy of its bottle's design.

A common myth is that tequila bottles house a worm. The 'worm' is actually a butterfly that, in its larval stage, can live in certain types of agave. The larva has long been known to be a nutritional source of food. One day a manufacturer decided to put one in a bottle with the idea that the living

all you need to create a decent margarita is good-quality tequila, orange-flavoured liqueur and limes

larva would ward off any evil spirits. This fascinated the outside world, which began to consume the larva on finishing the bottle for this reason but no doubt also due to the worm's reputed aphrodisiac quality!

And so, to the good stuff – you've sat patiently through the theory class but you'll have noticed that this is a book about the cocktails. Originally, the book started as a margaritas-only zone but during the research for the book (aahh the research) I came across a number of tequila-based gems, and during a little experimentation period (mmmm experimentation) I realized that tequila was a game and surprisingly versatile ingredient when it came to substituting it for other spirits in different classic cocktails. This said, there will always be similarities in the formulas used in tequila cocktails (look at the balance of sweet versus sour).

The margarita hasn't changed much over the years. It has survived numerous nips and tucks to retain its fierce identity. All you need to create a decent margarita is good-quality tequila, limes and orange-flavoured liqueur (preferably a reputable brand like Cointreau).

The trick with making margaritas for others is asking the correct questions: 'On the rocks or straight up?', 'With a salt rim or without?' and most importantly 'How do you like yours?'. In a perfect world, everyone should have the opportunity to order and receive a personalized margarita. Sadly this isn't practical in a busy bar, but there's no excuse not to experiment at home. Within the boundaries of the three ingredients used in the margarita there are a number of ways to make the resultant drink taste different.

The first and most obvious way to alter the taste of your drink is to try different brands and ages of tequila. Secondly, experiment with your choice of sour: Do you use freshly squeezed lime juice? Do you use sour mix? (Not if you can help it – I certainly wouldn't recommend it.) Thirdly, vary the type of sweetener. Triple sec is the most obvious choice but if you want to upgrade your margarita, try using Cointreau or Grand Marnier to create a richer concoction. Finally, think about the ratio of tequila to sour and sweet. Any combination of these variables will result in a very different taste.

With luck the following pages will stimulate your taste buds and curiosity alike. Tequila has proved to be a worthy travel companion over the last six months of writing. Here's hoping it proves itself worthy of your time.

cocktail basics

Equipment

The first thing any aspiring bartender should acquire is a *measure* (jigger). The modern dual-measure jigger measures both 50 ml/2 oz. and 25 ml/1 oz. (a double and a single measure). It is essential when mixing these recipes for the first time to follow the guidelines. The *shaker* is the second most important piece of equipment for a bartender. Also very important when dealing with the margarita is a *blender*. Little tip: When using a blender only use crushed ice (wrap ice in a clean dishcloth or bag and hit it with a rolling pin!) this will preserve the blender's blades. The *barspoon*, with its long spiralling handle,

is useful for stirring drinks and for the gentle pouring required for layered drinks. The 'wrong', flat end can be used for muddling or crushing herbs, etc. A *muddler* is a wooden pestle for mixing or crushing sugar cubes, limes and herbs, etc. A *mixing glass* with strainer is used for making drinks that are stirred, not shaken.

Glasses

The margarita can be served in a number of different glasses; either in a *rocks glass* if served on the rocks or in a *margarita coupette* (or in some instances a *martini glass*) if served straight up. Frozen margaritas tend to need slightly larger glasses, a *hurricane glass*

should be large enough. The *highball* should be at least 300 ml/10 oz. The *shot glass* comes in a number of shapes and sizes, any is acceptable. When selecting a rocks glass, I tend to prefer those with a thick base and heavy solid feel. The margarita glass can be as ornate or as basic as you see fit. You can frost your serving glasses by leaving them in the freezer for an hour before use.

Techniques

There are six basic ways of creating a cocktail: shaking, blending, stirring over ice, layering, building and muddling. Whichever method you are using, accurately measure the ingredients first to get that all-important balance of tastes

right. If you would rather try guesswork just see how much practice it takes to get the quantity right to fill the glass exactly.

Shaking is a more aggressive way to combine ingredients and should be treated as such – so put your back into it. Add the ingredients to the shaker and fill it with ice. The shaking movement should be sharp and fairly assertive, but do remember to keep your hands on both parts of the shaker or at least a finger on the cap. Five or six aggressive shakes should be enough to frost the shaker (a sign that the drink is ready). Drinks containing cream and juices should be either shaken for slightly longer than the usual ten seconds or blended.

Blending involves pouring all the ingredients into a blender, adding crushed ice and flicking the switch. *Stirring* is the best method when you want to retain the clarity and strength of the spirits. Use an ice-filled mixing glass and stir carefully to avoid chipping the ice and diluting the drink. *Layering* is the technique used for drinks such as La Cucaracha (page 60). With the flat end of a barspoon resting on the surface of the base spirit, pour each of the remaining spirits in turn down the handle of the spoon. This keeps the ingredients separate and allows them to be tasted one at a time.

The process of *building* a cocktail just requires adding the measured ingredients to the appropriate glass, with ice, and giving it a quick stir before serving. The *muddling* technique involves using the flat end of a barspoon or a muddler to mix or crush ingredients such as fruit or herbs and allow the flavours to be released gently.

Extras

For a *salt-rimmed* glass, simply wipe a lime around the rim of the glass. Rub the glass face down in a bowl of salt. Holding the glass upside down wipe the inside with a napkin to ensure the salt only coats the outside of the rim, and doesn't drop in to the drink. For a *lime* or *orange zest*, take a sharp knife and gently skim a length of peel from the fruit – the zest should be fine with no pith. Squeeze the zest over the drink, wipe it around the rim and then drop it into the liquid. To make *sugar syrup* stir 500 g/1 lb of sugar into 250 ml/1 cup of water and bring to the boil, stirring vigorously. Leave to cool. One last consideration is the *ice* you will be using to chill your cocktails. Where possible use large, dry ice cubes. If you want to go one step further use mineral water.

the originals

The margarita is a classic cocktail that has been around since the first half of the last century – that much is known. However, as is generally the case with cocktails, there is some confusion as to who exactly invented the drink. Each version of events sounds plausible enough but I am sure that no one was taking notes! Take your pick from the possibilities opposite – my advice would be to choose the story you find the most romantic.

sames
Hacienda in Acapulco, Mexico, c.1948.

Margarita Sames, an American socialite, wanted to impress her celebrity friends (including John Wayne) at a party. She mixed tequila with lime then added some of her favourite liqueur, Cointreau.

negrete
Garci Crespo Hotel in Pueblo, Mexico, 1936.

Danny Negrete created the margarita with a salt rim for his girlfriend. The young lady had a passion for dipping her fingers into salt but knew it didn't look good! This was quite a novel idea at the time.

herrera
Rancho La Gloria Bar, Rosarito Beach, Tijuana, Mexico, 1938.

Bar owner Danny Herrera created the drink for a showgirl, Marjorie King, who was allergic to all spirits except tequila. He named his creation margarita, the Spanish version of Marjorie.

derlesse & underwood
Tail o' the Cock, Los Angeles, USA, c.1950.

The margarita was made popular at the Tail o' the Cock by a young bartender, Derlesse. When Vernon Underwood, president of Cuervo Tequila distribution, discovered that the margarita was responsible for a huge increase in Cuervo sales, he began to market the drink.

morales
Tommy's Place, El Paso, Texas, USA, 1942.

Bartender Pancho Morales, created the margarita when asked to mix a Magnolia. Unsure of the exact recipe, Morales made one up, adding tequila and lime to Cointreau. Keeping with the flower theme, he named the drink margarita – the Spanish word for daisy.

classic margaritas

All you need to create a margarita is good-quality tequila, lime and orange-flavoured liqueur. Yet within the boundaries of these ingredients you can make your drink taste quite different. The type of tequila, the choice of sour, the brand of sweetener and the ratio of all three influence the final flavour. There is no such thing as the perfect margarita and the only person who can judge the levels of perfection is its recipient. Here are some simple recipes to get you started on the road of experimentation.

standard

50 ml/2 oz. gold tequila

25 ml/1 oz. triple sec

25 ml/1 oz. fresh lime juice

lime wheel, to garnish

salt (for the glass)

sames

25 ml/1 oz. gold tequila

25 ml/1 oz. Cointreau

25 ml/1 oz. fresh lime juice

lime wheel, to garnish

salt (for the glass)

strong

50 ml/2 oz. tequila

25 ml/1 oz. Grand Marnier

25 ml/1 oz. fresh lime juice

lime wheel, to garnish

salt (for the glass)

Add all the ingredients to a shaker filled with ice. Shake sharply and strain into a salt-rimmed, frosted margarita glass. Garnish with a lime wheel.
OR
For frozen margaritas, add all the ingredients to a blender, add one scoop of crushed ice and blend for 20 seconds. Pour into a margarita coupette and garnish with a lime wheel.

the premium margaritas

Depending on the method of production and age, tequila yields an abundance of different flavours. This chapter includes some of my favourite fine tequila brands mixed with a delicate balance of sour and sweetness. From the sensational 200th anniversary José Cuervo Reserva de la Familia tequila, used in the 24 Carat Gold Reserva (page 28), to the quality Patrón Añejo found in La Margarita de le Patrón (opposite), you will discover just how the brand of tequila can influence the taste of your margarita. Each of the tequila brands used in this chapter should be readily available in most specialist liquor shops.

la margarita de le patrón

Patrón stands up as a tequila to be counted. But be warned, its decanter-type bottle may have upped the price on this top end tequila. Mixed with Citronage (a premium orange liqueur), this margarita is the drink you'd choose if money were no object.

50 ml/2 oz. Patrón Añejo tequila
35 ml/1¼ oz. Citronage
25 ml/1 oz. fresh lime juice
salt (for the glass)

Add all the ingredients to a shaker filled with ice. Shake sharply and strain into a salt-rimmed, frosted margarita coupette.

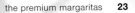

horny toad

Made using Sauza Hornitos, the Horny Toad is named after the creature used to exemplify ugliness in Mexico. Are they saying drinking tequila makes you unattractive? (I've always found everyone much more attractive when I've been drinking tequila!)

50 ml/2 oz. Sauza Hornitos tequila
25 ml/1 oz. Cointreau
35 ml/1¼ oz. fresh lime juice
lime wedge, to garnish
salt (for the glass)

Add all the ingredients to a shaker filled with ice. Shake sharply and strain into a salt-rimmed, rocks glass filled with ice. Garnish with a lime wedge.

conmemorativo triple triple

50 ml/2 oz. Sauza
Conmemorativo tequila

25 ml/1 oz. Cointreau

35 ml/1¼ oz. fresh
lemon juice

salt (for the glass)

Triple-distilled Cointreau and triple-distilled Sauza Conmemorativo, mixed with freshly squeezed lemon juice, provides the balance this cocktail requires. Sauza Conmemorativo was introduced to the market as the demand for premium tequila rose – it's a great sign that drinkers are beginning to appreciate the value of fine tequila.

Add all the ingredients to a shaker filled with ice. Shake sharply and strain into a salt-rimmed, frosted martini glass.

porfidio single barrel perfecta

Porfidio has long been a much-coveted tequila, predominantly due to the beauty of its designer bottles. The skilfully handblown bottle shows off a glass saguaro cactus standing inside (which does nothing to upturn the myth that tequila is made from cactus!). In fairness, the tequila they make is rather good too.

50 ml/2 oz. Porfidio Single Barrel tequila

25 ml/1 oz. Cointreau

25 ml/1 oz. fresh lemon juice

salt (for the glass)

Add all the ingredients to a shaker filled with ice. Shake sharply and strain into a frosted margarita glass.

lo mayor de sauza

Sauza are the second biggest tequila producers in the world and the Galardon Gran Reposado gives us a reason to understand why. Delicious!

50 ml/2 oz. Sauza Galardon Gran Reposado tequila

25 ml/1 oz. Cointreau

25 ml/1 oz. fresh lime juice

lime wedge, to garnish

salt (for the glass)

Add all the ingredients to a shaker filled with ice. Shake sharply and strain into a salt-rimmed rocks glass.

24 carat gold reserva

200th anniversary José Cuervo Gran Reserva de la Familia is one of my favourite sipping tequilas, and it would seem sacrilegious to mix it with anything other than the 150th anniversary cuvée Speciale Centcinqantenaire Grand Marnier.

50 ml/2 oz. José Cuervo Reserva de la Familia tequila

35 ml/1¼ oz. Centcinqantenaire Grand Marnier

35 ml/1¼ oz. fresh lime juice

salt (for the glass)

Add all the ingredients to a shaker filled with ice. Shake sharply and strain into a frosted margarita glass.

boogie man

This drink's name alludes to a fear that I have heard about many times when it comes to drinking tequila, but we all know the boogie man's not real, right?

50 ml/2 oz. Chamucos tequila

25 ml/1 oz. Cointreau

25 ml/1 oz. fresh lime juice

salt (for the glass)

Add all the ingredients to a shaker filled with ice. Shake sharply and strain into a salt-rimmed, frosted margarita glass.

the flavoureds

Bartenders have been adding all sorts of flavours to cocktails for decades and the margarita is no exception. The margarita is quite a finely balanced cocktail, so don't be too rash with your creativity. Adding fresh fruit to cocktails is always more authentic than using fruit liqueurs but two things need to be kept in mind when doing so. First, the ripest fruit will yield the most flavoursome results; secondly, it is important when using strongly flavoured fruits not to overshadow the taste of the tequila.

diablo

A long refreshing cocktail with a delicate hint of blackcurrant.

50 ml/2 oz. gold tequila
15 ml/½ oz. fresh lime
15 ml/½ oz. crème de cassis
ginger ale
redcurrants, to garnish

Build all the ingredients in a hurricane glass filled with crushed ice. Garnish with a small bunch of redcurrants and serve with two straws.

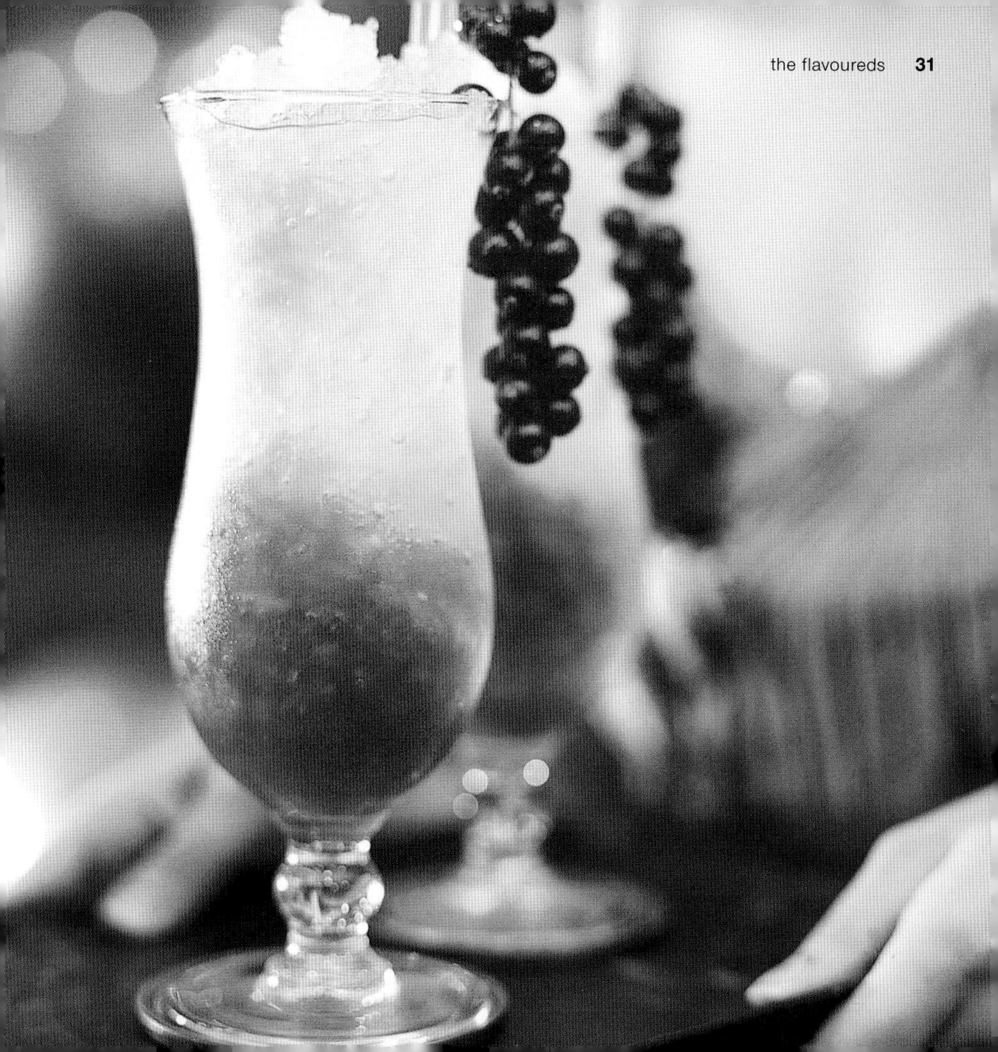

hibiscus margarita

20 ml/scant oz.
hibiscus cordial

50 ml/2 oz. **Cuervo
Gold tequila**

20 ml/scant oz. **triple sec**

20 ml/scant oz.
fresh lime juice

Hibiscus cordial

500 g/2¼ cups sugar

100 g/4 oz. **hibiscus
flowers**

A deep-purple margarita with the gentle essence of herbed sweetness from the hibiscus. Worth the effort if you aim to impress.

Hibiscus cordial: Dissolve the sugar and hibiscus flowers (dried if out of season) into 2 litres/quarts of water on a low heat. Once the liquid turns a deep red, strain and leave to cool.

Add all the ingredients to a shaker filled with ice. Shake sharply and strain into a large cocktail glass.

raspberry torte

A successful cocktail needs to have an effect on all of your cocktail senses. This one looks great on the eye, has a fresh lime and berry fragrance on the nose and, if you can ever bring yourself to consume your work of art, delights the tastebuds.

50 ml/2 oz.
gold tequila

20 ml/scant oz.
Cointreau

20 ml/scant oz.
fresh lime juice

50 ml/2 oz.
raspberry purée

Blend the first three ingredients in a blender with two scoops of crushed ice for 20 seconds. Pour half the mixture into a margarita glass. Gently layer the purée over the surface of the drink to create a thin red line. Add the remaining margarita mix over the top and serve with two straws.

mangorita

This cocktail is an easy one to make, but very tricky to get right. Mango is a powerful-tasting fruit, which can overshadow the taste of tequila entirely, so take care not to add too much mango, especially if it is very ripe.

50 ml/2 oz. gold tequila

20 ml/scant oz. triple sec

20 ml/scant oz. fresh lime juice

25 ml/1 oz. mango purée (or ½ peeled mango)

a mango slice, to garnish

Add all the ingredients to a blender. Add two scoops of crushed ice and blend for 20 seconds. Pour into a margarita coupette and garnish with a slice of fresh mango.

pinarita

The combination of pineapple and tequila results in a truly tropical flavour. I will allow you to decorate it lavishly despite my open disdain for garish garnishes!

50 ml/2 oz. gold tequila

20 ml/scant oz. triple sec

20 ml/scant oz. fresh lime juice

25 ml/1 oz. pineapple juice

thin slice of fresh pineapple, plus 1 to garnish

Add all the ingredients to a blender. Add two scoops of crushed ice and blend for 20 seconds. Pour into a margarita coupette, garnish with a pineapple slice and serve with two straws.

green iguana

The combination of melon and tequila works perfectly here. I have chosen to use Midori (a melon-flavoured liqueur) in this recipe, as fresh melon doesn't have the necessary sweetness to balance the drink.

50 ml/2 oz. Sauza Hornitos tequila
25 ml/1 oz. Midori
25 ml/1 oz. fresh lime juice

Add all the ingredients to a shaker filled with ice. Shake sharply and strain into a rocks glass filled with ice.

triple gold margarita

50 ml/2 oz. gold tequila

10 ml/2 barspoons Cointreau

10 ml/2 barspoons Grand Marnier

20 ml/scant oz. fresh lime juice

10 ml/2 barspoons Goldschlager

Layered with a float of Goldschlager, the Triple Gold Margarita will bring a touch of splendour to any bar menu. Laced with real 24 carat gold pieces, Goldschlager is a cinnamon-flavoured liqueur that adds considerably to the depth of taste of the cocktail.

Add all the ingredients except the Goldschlager to a shaker filled with ice. Shake sharply and strain into a frosted margarita glass. Float the Goldschlager onto the surface of the mixture and serve.

tres compadres

The combination of lime, orange and grapefruit juice provide the three citrus compadres. Cointreau and Chambord are then added to the mix to sweeten, and lo and behold a great cocktail is born. Try serving this long (by adding more orange and grapefruit juice) for an extra-refreshing cooler.

50 ml/2 oz. Sauza Conmemorativo tequila

20 ml/scant oz. Cointreau

20 ml/scant oz. Chambord

25 ml/1 oz. fresh lime juice

20 ml/scant oz. orange juice

20 ml/scant oz. grapefruit juice

a lime wedge, to garnish

salt, for the glass

Add all the ingredients to a shaker filled with ice. Shake sharply and strain into a chilled margarita glass edged with salt. Garnish with a lime wedge.

red cactus

The fresh raspberries and Chambord in this drink team up to provide a fruity punch that almost masks the flavour of its base spirit. Don't be deceived; there's still plenty of tequila in here.

50 ml/2 oz. Sauza Extra Gold tequila

20 ml/scant oz. triple sec

20 ml/scant oz. Chambord

35 ml/1¼ oz. fresh lime juice

4 fresh raspberries, plus 2 to garnish

a lime wedge, to garnish

Add all the ingredients to a blender. Add two scoops of crushed ice and blend for 20 seconds. Pour into a margarita coupette or hurricane glass. Garnish with a lime wedge and serve with two raspberries.

berry margarita

50 ml/2 oz. gold tequila

20 ml/scant oz. triple sec

20 ml/scant oz. fresh lime juice

dash of crème de mure

seasonal berries of your choice, plus extra to garnish

Anything from strawberries to cranberries, blueberries to raspberries can be used in this recipe. Choose your own combination of seasonal berries for subtle variations.

Add all the ingredients to a blender. Add two scoops of crushed ice and blend for 20 seconds. Pour into a margarita coupette and garnish with a berry.

prickly pear margarita

The prickly pear has become *de rigueur* in cocktails and makes a great addition to the margarita. The average pear doesn't always contain enough flavour to carry the drink off so it's well worth spending that bit of extra time looking for the prickly pears.

50 ml/2 oz. silver tequila

20 ml/scant oz. triple sec

20 ml/scant oz. lime juice

dash of grenadine

25 ml/1 oz. prickly pear purée

thin slice of pear, to garnish

Add all the ingredients to a shaker filled with ice. Shake sharply and strain into a frosted margarita glass. Garnish with a sliver of pear.

habañero margarita

This is a drink that I have dabbled with over the years. The first batch I made was served with a glass of milk on the side and an apologetic look on my face. Now I serve it with confidence. Moral of the story: get your mix right before serving and don't leave your peppers infusing for too long!

Habañero infusion

3 habañero peppers, plus 1 to garnish

bottle of gold tequila

50 ml/2 oz. habañero–infused gold tequila

25 ml/1 oz. Cointreau

25 ml/1 oz. fresh lime juice

Habañero infusion: Add three fresh habañero peppers to a bottle of gold tequila. Leave for two days or until the peppers lose their colour.

Add all the ingredients to a shaker filled with ice. Shake sharply and strain into a frosted margarita glass. Garnish with a habañero pepper.

blue moon

I'm not a man to hold grudges but I'm not a huge fan of blue cocktails, they tend to contain blue Curaçao for its colour rather than its taste. In the Blue Moon, however, blue Curaçao is valid, as the liqueur is orange-flavoured, much like triple sec.

50 ml/2 oz. Sauza Hornitos tequila

25 ml/1 oz. blue Curaçao

15 ml/½ oz. fresh lime juice

2 scoops lemon sorbet

Add all the ingredients to a blender. Blend for 20 seconds and pour into a margarita glass.

the
substitutions

Substituting the spirit in a tried and tested recipe is a great way to discover a new drink. Tequila has the ability to lend a great deal to a cocktail – try using an aged tequila for an even more complex spectrum of flavours. When experimenting with this method ask yourself the following questions: Does the drink mix well with cream? What balance of citrus and sweet tastes best? What other ingredients work well with the spirit?

herba buena

This is a variation on the Cuban classic, the Mojito. Pack the glass with crushed ice and this cocktail makes the perfect summer drink. Add a little extra sugar for the sweeter tooth or a little more lime for that citrus twist.

50 ml/2 oz. gold tequila
15 ml/½ oz. fresh lime juice
brown rock sugar cube
5 mint sprigs, plus 1 to garnish
soda water

Muddle all the ingredients apart from the soda in a highball glass using a bonzer spoon. Add crushed ice, muddle again and top up with soda. Stir gently, garnish with a mint sprig and serve with two straws.

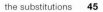

conmemorativo

The Conmemorativo is a rustic variation on the margarita, using a premium, aged tequila. It was a New York band, the Fun Lovin' Criminals, who (during a night at the Met Bar in London) suggested that this special tequila could be used in a cocktail just as long as it was shown respect.

1 lime
2 white sugar cubes
50 ml/2 oz. Sauza Conmemorativo tequila

Cut the lime into eighths, squeeze and place in a salt-edged old-fashioned glass with the sugar, then pound well with a muddler. Top up with crushed ice, add the tequila, stir and serve.

rude cosmopolitan

35 ml/1¼ oz. gold tequila
20 ml/scant oz. triple sec
25 ml/1 oz. cranberry juice
20 ml/scant oz. fresh lime juice
orange zest, to garnish

This drink earned its name following an evening that began well enough but descended into heated debate. The tone of the evening changed when they started to drink tequila – hence the drink's name.

Shake all the ingredients well over ice and strain into a chilled martini glass. Garnish with orange zest.

tequilini

Based on the martini, this cocktail is a great way to serve an aged tequila. Chilled to perfection and softened by the vermouth – sip and savour your Tequilini.

dash dry vermouth

50 ml/2 oz. premium añejo tequila

lime zest, to garnish

Add a dash of vermouth to a mixing glass filled with ice. Stir gently then discard any dilution. Add the tequila and stir again for fifteen seconds. Strain the mixture into a frosted martini glass and garnish with a thin zest of lime.

mezcal margarita

Choosing to substitute mezcal for tequila will impress any bartender. Mezcal tends to be more herbaceous and earthy on the palate – taste this drink and you'll find yourself whipped off to Mexico.

50 ml/2 oz. mezcal

2 dashes of Peychaud's Bitters (or Angostura)

20 ml/scant oz. triple sec

20 ml/scant oz. fresh lime juice

salt (for the glass)

Add all the ingredients to a shaker filled with ice. Shake sharply and strain into a salt-rimmed frosted margarita glass.

añejo manhattan

The Manhattan can be made sweet, perfect or dry depending on the ratio of sweet and dry vermouth. This is the perfect version. Try using all sweet or all dry vermouth instead.

50 ml/2 oz. añejo tequila

20 ml/scant oz. sweet vermouth

20 ml/scant oz. dry vermouth

dash of Angostura bitters

orange zest, to garnish

Add all the ingredients to a mixing glass filled with ice. Using a bonzer spoon, stir in a continuous motion until the mixture is thoroughly chilled. Strain into a frosted martini glass and garnish with orange zest.

tequila colada

This variation slips down the throat as easily as its name rolls off the tongue. Ensure this drink has the right consistency (light and fluffy) by adding crushed ice bit by bit to the blender.

50 ml/2 oz. gold tequila

20 ml/scant oz. coconut cream

10 ml/2 barspoons double/heavy cream

150 ml/⅔ cup pineapple juice

pineapple slice, to garnish

Add all the ingredients to a blender with two scoops of crushed ice. Blend for 20 seconds. Pour into a hurricane glass and garnish with a pineapple slice.

lagerita

A fave of mine, this is a drink for the more adventurous among us. It is essential that a dark beer is used. Apologies for the vulgarity of the name but the temptation was too great!!

1 lime

25 ml/1 oz. Centenario Añejo tequila

brown rock sugar cube

Negra Modello, or other dark beer

Cut the lime into quarters, squeeze and drop them into a highball glass. Add the tequila and the sugar cube and muddle using a bar spoon. Fill the glass with ice and add the dark beer. Muddle again ensuring as much of the sugar has dissolved as possible. Serve with two straws.

bloody maria

If ever I find the need for solace in a hangover cure, the Maria is a worthy adversary to the Mary. Where the vodka in a Mary thins the mixture slightly, the tequila in a Maria binds the ingredients.

50 ml/2 oz. gold tequila

20 ml/scant oz. fresh lime juice

250 ml/1 cup tomato juice

5 dashes of Tabasco sauce

5 dashes of Worcestershire sauce

pinch of sea salt

pinch of ground black pepper

pinch of celery salt

lime wedge, to garnish

celery stick, to garnish

Add all the ingredients to a shaker filled with ice. Shake sharply and strain into a highball glass filled with ice. Garnish with a lime wedge and celery.

other tequila cocktails

Tequila has been mixed in traditional Mexican drinks and western variations for years. Some you may love, others you may not thank me for reminding you of. Try the Three Amigos for tequila at its most basic, a Submarine for tequila at its laziest or a Silk Stocking for tequila at its most decadent. The method of consumption can be as fun as the effect of the drink itself.

salty chihuahua

This is a tequila variation on the Salty Dog. It's a simple combination that can cut through the fog of any hangover. Try adding a dash of hibiscus cordial for a sweetened variation.

50 ml/2 oz. tequila

200 ml/¾ cup pink grapefruit juice

a lime wedge, to garnish

salt, for the glass

Pour the tequila into a salt-edged highball glass filled with ice. Top with the grapefruit juice, garnish with a lime wedge and serve.

los tres amigos

The salt, tequila and lime method is as ubiquitous as the margarita when it comes to tequila. Recite the immortal words: 'lick, sip, suck' – and enjoy!

lime wedge

50 ml/2 oz. gold tequila

pinch of salt

Hold the lime wedge between the thumb and index finger. Pour the tequila into a shot glass and place the glass in the fleshy part of your hand between the same thumb and finger. Place a pinch of salt onto the top of your hand next to the shot glass. In this order; lick the salt, shoot the tequila, and suck on the lime.

submarine

Forget those age-old constraints of spirit and chaser standing alone. Opt instead for the energy-saving Submarine and allow the tequila to seep gently from under its upturned shot glass and mingle with the beer before it hits the palate.

50 ml/2 oz. gold tequila

bottle Mexican beer (Sol)

Pour the tequila into a shot glass. Place the shot glass into an inverted beer glass so that it touches the base of the beer glass. Turn the beer glass the right way up so that the shot glass is upside down but the tequila is still inside. Gently fill the beer glass with the beer and serve.

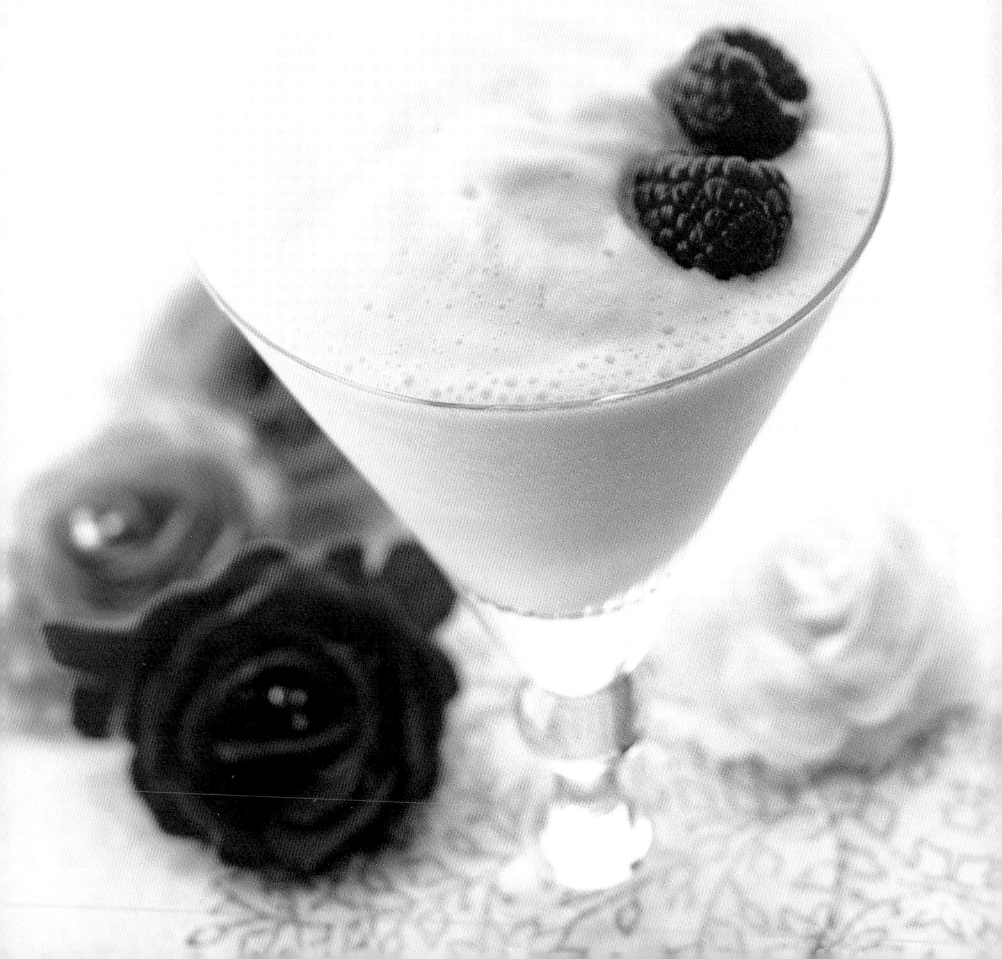

silk stocking

This tequila drink was invented during the '20s in the US, at a time when cocktails were often given names revelling in innuendo and sensuality.

Add all the ingredients to a blender. Add two scoops of crushed ice and blend for 20 seconds. Pour the mixture into a hurricane glass, garnish with two raspberries and serve with two straws.

35 ml/1¼ oz. gold tequila

15 ml/½ oz. white crème de cacao

5 ml/1 barspoon grenadine

15 ml/½ oz. double/heavy cream

2 fresh raspberries, to garnish

the sangrita

This drink is the perfect way to savour a fine tequila. Try varying the Sangrita mix, by adding different amounts of orange juice and spices.

Pour the tequila into a shot glass. Add the remaining ingredients to a separate shot glass and stir gently. This drink should be tasted tequila first, followed by the Sangrita mix.

50 ml/2 oz. añejo tequila

Sangrita mix

25 ml/1 oz. orange juice

25 ml/1 oz. lime juice

dash of grenadine

dash of Tabasco sauce

dash of Worcestershire sauce

moppet

Although some may say this wicked combination has had its day, you'll agree it's a great way to start an evening with a fizz and a bang. Place a napkin over the glass and swirl the drink, reciting the traditional chant 'un, dos, tres, voom!' before slamming.

50 ml/2 oz. silver tequila
50 ml/2 oz. lemonade/lemon soda

Pour both ingredients into a rocks glass. Cover the glass with a paper napkin and slam onto a firm surface. Quickly, while the drink is fizzing, drink the mixture. Alternatively, substitute with gold tequila and champagne.

la cucaracha

After creating the perfectly layered shot, La Cucaracha needs to be lit (use a warm glass) and consumed through a straw (from bottom up).

Layer the spirits one on top of the other using the flat end of a barspoon. Place a straw into the mixture and light the surface liquid. The drink must be drunk before the flame melts the straw.

15 ml/½ oz. kahlua
15 ml/½ oz. tequila
15 ml/½ oz. over-proof rum (Wray & Nephew)

el chupacabre

Translated as 'the vampire', the addition of garlic is perhaps unsurprising. Try using gently crushed garlic cloves and freshly ground chillies for extra zing. It's worth playing around with the strengths of the various ingredients before serving to an unsuspecting public.

Shake all the ingredients in a shaker filled with ice and strain through a sieve into a highball glass filled with ice. Garnish with a sprig of fresh mint.

50 ml/2 oz. gold tequila

200 ml/¾ cup tomato juice

1 tablespoon medium hot red chilli purée, or 2 tablespoons salsa or pico de gallo

20 ml/scant oz. fresh lime juice

large pinch of garlic powder

large pinch of sea salt

fresh mint sprigs, to garnish

tequila sunrise

A cocktail synonymous with the '70s, bad hair, lava lamps and cheesy cocktails. Try modernizing the recipe using Chambord instead of the grenadine for more depth. Alternatively swallow your pride, slip into your flairs and enjoy.

Build the tequila and the orange juice into a highball glass filled with ice. Gently pour the grenadine down the inside of the glass so the syrup fills the bottom. Garnish with a thin orange slice and serve with two straws.

50 ml/2 oz. gold tequila

20 ml/scant oz. grenadine

200 ml/¾ cup fresh orange juice

orange slice, to garnish

index